religion in focus
sikhism

Geoff Teece

W
FRANKLIN WATTS
LONDON•SYDNEY

First published in Great Britain by
Franklin Watts
96 Leonard Street
LONDON EC2A 4XD

Franklin Watts Australia
45–51 Huntley Street
Alexandria
NSW 2015

ISBN: 0 7496 4799 X

A CIP catalogue record for this book is available from the British Library

Printed in Malaysia

Series Editor: Adrian Cole
Designer: Proof Books
Art Director: Jonathan Hair
Consultant: Rajinder Singh Panesar
Picture Researcher: Diana Morris

Acknowledgements

The publishers would like to thank the following for
permission to reproduce photographs in this book:

Annie Griffiths Belt/Corbis: 9. David Cumming/Eye Ubiquitous: 8. Bennett Dean/Eye
Ubiquitous: 24. Chris Fairclough: back cover, 15, 20t, 28. Chris Lisle/Corbis: 11, 25. Buddy
Mays/Corbis: 17b. Bipin J. Mistry/Circa PL: 1, 6. Desai
Noshir/Corbis Sygma: 10. Richard
Olivier/Corbis: 29t. Christine
Osborne/Circa PL: 18t, 23, 30.
Christine Osborne/Corbis: 22t. Tim
Page/Eye Ubiquitous: 19. H Rogers/
Trip: front cover, 13t, 13c, 29b. Steve
Shott Photography: 18b, 27. John
Smith/Circa PL: 2, 3, 14, 17t, 22b.
Liba Taylor/Hutchison: 26. Twin
Studio/Circa PL: 5, 7.

Every attempt has been made to clear
copyright. Should there be any
inadvertent omission, please apply to
the publisher for rectification.

Contents

Origins of Sikhism

Sikhism is the youngest of the major religions and dates from the fifteenth century CE. The origins of Sikhism lie in the teachings of Guru Nanak and his successors. His life and teachings challenged many of the religious beliefs and practices of his time. He stressed devotion to God, service to others and the value of family life and hard work. The essence of Sikh teaching is summed up by Guru Nanak in these words: 'Realisation of Truth is higher than all else. Higher still is truthful living.'

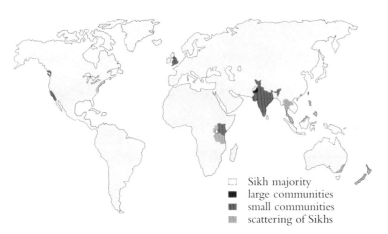

☐ Sikh majority
■ large communities
▥ small communities
▨ scattering of Sikhs

SIKH POPULATION

Today there are about 16 million Sikhs worldwide. There are communities in the United States, Canada, the UK, Singapore, East Africa, Malaysia and Hong Kong. However, 80 per cent of Sikhs live in the Punjab in India. Some Sikhs believe that the Punjab should become an independent homeland called Khalistan (the land of the pure).

GURU NANAK'S EARLY LIFE

Guru Nanak's life is recorded in a group of stories called the *Janam Sakhis*. Guru Nanak, the first Sikh Guru, was born on 15 April 1469, in Talwandi, a village in the western Punjab region of India. He was born into a Hindu family and had many Hindu and Muslim friends. Nanak was a clever child who studied Hindi and mathematics, as well as Muslim literature. When Nanak reached the age of 13 he was due to be invested with the sacred thread, a traditional Hindu custom that represents the 'coming of age'. However, to the disappointment of his family, Nanak refused the thread. He sang these words: 'Let mercy be the cotton, contentment the thread, continence the knot and truth the twist.' This was an early sign of Nanak's future teachings which say that values and 'truthful living' are more important than religious rituals.

MARRIED LIFE

The *Janam Sakhis* record that Nanak spent much of his time as a youth discussing spiritual matters with Hindu and Muslim holy men. To make Nanak concentrate more on everyday responsibilities, a suitable girl was found for him. He became happily married at the age of 16 and later had two children. He found that married life did not interfere with his spiritual concerns. During the day he worked as an accountant. At night, and in the early mornings, he meditated and sang *shabads*, or hymns, accompanied by his friend Mardana who was a musician.

NANAK'S CALL

Years later, Nanak disappeared one morning after going down to the river. He had gone to talk with God. God taught him the *Mool Mantra* (see page 16), a verse which begins: 'There is but One God. He is all-pervading. His name is everlasting.' These words are found at the beginning of the Sikh scriptures, the *Guru Granth Sahib* (see pages 14–15).

All of Nanak's friends and family assumed that he had drowned. They were amazed when he reappeared three days later! However, Nanak had been spiritually transformed and he shone with a divine light. He said nothing – he seemed to be in a trance. He gave up his job and distributed all of his possessions to the poor. When he finally broke his silence he uttered the memorable words: 'There is no Hindu, no Muslim'. When asked by a Muslim to explain this he said: 'Let God's grace be the mosque, and devotion the prayer mat. Let the Qur'an be good conduct.'

These words represent an important Sikh teaching: all human beings are children of God even though they follow different religions. What Nanak's teachings gave the Sikh tradition is a belief that it is important to be good, or true.

NANAK THE TEACHER

Nanak travelled to spread his message. He went all over the Far and Middle East, eventually returning to Kartharpur in the Punjab where he settled down with his wife and family. Devotees came to listen to his teachings, gathering in the mornings and afternoons for religious services.

Nanak believed in a casteless society, without any distinctions between rich and poor, birthright, sex or religion. He began the communal kitchen called *langar*, which is a fundamental practice for all Sikhs today. Just before Guru Nanak died he appointed Guru Angad, one of his most devoted followers, as his successor.

NANAK'S DEATH

Guru Nanak died on 22 September 1539. His Hindu and Muslim followers placed fresh flowers under the sheet that covered his body. Days later they lifted the sheet and found the flowers were still fresh. The Hindus took their flowers and cremated them, and the Muslims took theirs and buried them. Today, Sikhs normally cremate their dead.

GURU NANAK
This illustration shows Guru Nanak (standing on the right) ordaining the second Guru.

HUMAN EQUALITY
Sikhs believe that to deny the authenticity of other religions is to question God's purpose. Therefore, as humans are equal, it is important for Sikhs to act in the service of all people. The third Guru, Guru Amar Das, is recorded as saying: 'All are created from the seed of God. There is the same clay in the whole world; the potter (God) makes many kinds of pots.'

The ten Gurus

THE TEN GURUS

Sikhs regard the Gurus with great reverence and believe they are inspired by God. Pictures often show the Gurus wearing haloes.

The same message as revealed originally to Guru Nanak, the first Guru, was passed on by the succession of ten Gurus.

GURU ANGAD (1504–52), THE SECOND GURU:

- started schools for children and women to learn the Gurmukhi script.
- wrote the first biography of Guru Nanak and gathered together some of the first Guru's *shabads* (hymns).
- extended the practice of *langar*, which Guru Nanak had begun.

Guru Angad was originally a Hindu called Lehna. He first met Guru Nanak at the age of 27. After meeting Guru Nanak, Lehna became a devout follower and was appointed as Guru Nanak's successor.

GURU AMAR DAS (1479–1574), THE THIRD GURU:

- appointed a devout Sikh in charge of each of 22 regions of the Punjab.
- gathered Sikhs together three times during the year at the Hindu festival times of *Baisakhi, Maghi* and *Diwali* in order to form a bond between Sikhs.

Amar Das became a Guru in 1552 at the age of 73. He was made Guru because of his selfless service and his great humility and wisdom.

GURU RAM DAS (1534–81), THE FOURTH GURU:

- founded Chack Ramdas P., a village which was renamed Amritsar in 1574.
- composed *shabads* including the *Lavan*, a four-verse hymn which now forms a central part of *Anand Karaj* (the marriage ceremony, see page 28).

Guru Ram Das was installed as Guru at the age of 40. He continued to spread the Sikh faith.

GURU ARJAN (1563–1606), THE FIFTH GURU:

- completed the building of Amritsar, including the Harmandir Sahib.
- compiled the *Adi Granth* (the first version of the *Guru Granth Sahib*). The *Adi Granth* included the *shabads* of the first four Gurus and Guru Arjan's own hymns.

Arjan became Guru in 1581, just before the death of his father, Guru Ram Das. He became the first Sikh martyr when he was tortured and killed in 1606 on the orders of the Mughal Emperor Jahangir.

GURU HARGOBIND (1595–1644), THE SIXTH GURU:

- organised Sikhs to defend the weak and helpless. Instead of wearing prayer beads he began wearing two *Kirpans* (swords); one symbolised spiritual power, and the other worldly authority. These two *Kirpans* now form part of the Sikh symbol the *Khanda*.

Guru Hargobind was the son of Guru Arjan and succeeded him in 1606. After the murder (martyrdom) of his father, he realised that the Sikh community and other non-Muslim communities had to defend the right to practise their faith.

GURU HAR RAI (1630–61), THE SEVENTH GURU:

- Guru Har Rai, the grandson of Guru Hargobind, provided free medical aid to the needy, a practice that is now a common feature of gurdwaras in India.

GURU HAR KRISHAN (1656–64), THE EIGHTH GURU:

Guru Har Krishan, the son of Guru Har Rai, was only five years old when he became a Guru. He had been a Guru for only three years when he died from smallpox after tending the sick.

GURU TEGH BAHADUR (1621–75), THE NINTH GURU:

- agreed to help Hindus facing Mughal persecution, but was imprisoned and eventually died.

Guru Tegh Bahadur was Guru from 1664–1675 and was the youngest son of Guru Hargobind. His time as Guru coincided with Mughal persecution of Hindus. Guru Tegh Bahadur was the second Sikh martyr.

GURU GOBIND SINGH (1666–1708), THE TENTH GURU:

- organised Sikhs into a more effective military force.
- created the *Khalsa* (see pages 10–11).
- established *Amrit Sanskar* (see page 11).

On the death of Guru Tegh Bahadur, Guru Gobind Singh became the tenth and final human Guru. The Mughal persecutions were continuing and Gobind Singh felt the need to organise Sikhs into a more effective military force. It was at this time that the notion of a Sikh being a soldier saint was born. Before Guru Gobind Singh died, he announced that there would be no more human Gurus and that the Sikh teacher would be the holy scripture – the *Guru Granth Sahib* (see pages 14–15).

GURU GOBIND SINGH
Guru Gobind Singh was the tenth and final human Guru. He created the *Khalsa*.

The formation of Sikh tradition

From the death of Guru Gobind Singh until the end of the eighteenth century, Sikhs suffered persecution from the declining Muslim Mughal Empire of India. Despite the fact that Guru Gobind Singh was the last spiritual teacher, Sikhs still needed political leadership. Banda Singh became leader of the Sikhs after the last Guru's death and he tried to defend them against forced conversion to Islam. Eventually, in 1716, he was captured and taken to Delhi. He and six hundred members of his army were executed.

The Sikhs rallied together in 1799, when the Sikh armies led by Maharaja Ranjit Singh captured Lahore. This is an important time in Sikh history when the Punjab was one united country. All religions were respected and no one was seen as more important than the other.

Ranjit Singh is also remembered for developing the town of Amritsar, and the reconstruction of the Sikhs' holiest building called the Harmandir Sahib. The building became widely known as the 'Golden Temple' after Ranjit Singh had it decorated with gold leaf. He died in 1849. About ten years after his death the British, now established as a colonial power in India, took control of the Punjab.

AMRITSAR, INDIA

After the capture of Lahore in 1799, the town of Amritsar was developed by Ranjit Singh. He had the Harmandir Sahib decorated with gold leaf.

THE NINETEENTH CENTURY

Despite the good things achieved by Ranjit Singh, the dawning of the nineteenth century saw Sikhism in disarray. Many Sikh temples, called gurdwaras, came under Hindu control, which meant the *Guru Granth Sahib* shared the prayer hall with *murtis* (statues) of the Hindu deities, and marriages were conducted according to Hindu laws. This led to a Sikh religious revival. Three groups played a very significant part in forming the Sikh tradition as it is known today. These are the Nirankaris, the Namdharis and the Singh Sabha Movement.

THE NIRANKARIS

A spiritual leader called Dayal Das (1783–1855) reacted against the dominance of Hindu practices in gurdwaras. He encouraged Sikhs to hold their own naming and marriage ceremonies based around the *Guru Granth Sahib*. He revived the use of the Sikh wedding hymn called the *Lavan* and refused to let Hindu priests conduct Sikh weddings.

The Nirankari movement is so called because Dayal Das referred to God as Nirankar, which means 'the formless one'. He emphasised the spiritual teachings of Guru Nanak. He died in 1855.

THE NAMDHARIS

The spiritual leader Baba Ram Singh (1816–84) called for Sikhs to return to the basic spiritual and moral principles laid down by the Gurus. Some Sikhs had started smoking and drinking alcohol as well as charging large dowries. All this went against the teachings of the Gurus.

Some followers were executed by the British during the 1870s for trying to bring Sikh rule back to the Punjab.

THE SINGH SABHA MOVEMENT

This movement was established in 1873 to stop people from trying to convert Sikhs to Christianity or Hinduism. It placed a lot of emphasis on educational work, which resulted in the creation of Khalsa colleges.

Hindu deities were removed from gurdwaras. In the Punjab this led to the passing of the Gurdwara Act of 1925, which placed the Sikh places of worship back in the hands of Sikhs. The movement also led to consistency in practice. For example, Sikhs took part in *Amrit Sanskar* (initiation into the *Khalsa*) and wore the Panj Kakke (see pages 11–13).

USING COMPUTERS AT A KHALSA COLLEGE
Modern Khalsa colleges use a range of educational facilities. Much of the equipment is purchased with money from donations.

Khalsa and the Panj Kakke

PANJ PIARE

The Panj Piare were the first members of the *Khalsa*. The founding of the *Khalsa* is celebrated on *Baisakhi* (see page 23).

THE FOUNDING OF THE KHALSA

Guru Gobind Singh created the *Khalsa* (literally meaning 'pure') on *Baisakhi* Day, 30 March 1699, at Anandpur in the Punjab. Mughal leaders constantly threatened Sikhs and so Guru Gobind Singh called his followers together and asked who was strong enough to die for the faith. It is said that five volunteered and one by one accompanied the Guru into his tent. Each time the Guru reappeared with a bloodstained sword. After the fifth man had volunteered, the Guru reappeared with all five unharmed. They were, however, spiritually transformed by the experience and were given the title 'Panj Piare' (five beloved ones).

THE FIRST MEMBERS

Each of the five men were initiated into the *Khalsa* by the Guru in a ceremony known as *Amrit Sanskar*. This involved drinking *amrit* (water with sugar stirred by a double-edged sword called a *khanda*). Guru Gobind Singh sprinkled the *amrit* over the Panj Piare. They drank some of it and made vows of commitment to the faith. Afterwards the five initiated Guru Gobind Singh, who went on to initiate many thousands of men and women into the *Khalsa*. When the Guru conferred the title 'Singh' (which means 'lion') on men and 'Kaur' (which means 'princess') on women, he was using the terms to signify the Sikh teaching of equality. Among Hindus, people's caste could be identified by their name. For Sikhs, their identity was derived from their membership of the *Khalsa*, and not from where they were born or from their former caste. Therefore, the founding of the *Khalsa* reinforced the original teaching of Guru Nanak – that every human is equal.

THE AMRIT CEREMONY

Initiation into the *Khalsa* strengthens Sikhs' identity. Today, *Amrit Sanskar* usually takes place in a gurdwara and always in the presence of the *Guru Granth Sahib*. It is performed by five people who represent the original Panj Piare. The only ones allowed to witness the ceremony are the Panj Piare, those followers taking *amrit* and the person reading the *Guru Granth Sahib*.

Water and sugar are put into a steel bowl, called a *bata*, and stirred by a *khanda*, as in the original ceremony in 1699, while the Panj Piare recite five prayers. These include the *japji* of Guru Nanak. The Panj Piare and those followers taking *amrit* then kneel on the right knee and raise the left one. This symbolises that they are prepared to defend Sikhism. After the prayers, the followers drink some *amrit* from cupped hands and it is also sprinkled five times onto both eyes and into their hair. Sikhs who have been initiated into the *Khalsa* must wear the Panj Kakke (see pages 12–13).

AMRIT SANSKAR
During the ceremony, *amrit* is sprinkled over the follower as part of the initiation into the *Khalsa*.

KHALSA VOWS

In 1699, to signify their new identity, Sikhs began to wear the Panj Kakke (5 Ks) as symbols of their faith and commitment. They also took a number of vows. Those who commit themselves to the faith still keep these vows today, by taking part in the ceremony of *Amrit Sanskar*. These vows include a commitment to:

- not eat meat which has been slaughtered ritually
- follow the teachings of the Guru and serve the Guru, with weapons if necessary
- offer daily prayers
- give to charity
- reject all caste differences
- wear the Panj Kakke
- not remove hair from the body
- not take drugs or intoxicants
- respect all women and be faithful in marriage

THE PANJ KAKKE

THE PANJ KAKKE (5 Ks):
Kesh – uncut hair
Kanga – a wooden comb
Kara – a steel bracelet
Kirpan – a small sword
Kachera – underwear

The Panj Kakke (5 Ks) are very important Sikh symbols. Sikhs, both men and women, who are members of the *Khalsa* wear the Panj Kakke. The Panj Kakke are the single most visible symbols of Sikhism. They are not just a uniform. They remind Sikhs of various spiritual teachings and are seen as a powerful aid to living a truly Sikh lifestyle.

The Panj Kakke and their significance are:

KESH – uncut hair. Many people have traditionally shown their loyalties by wearing different tribal headdresses. The *Kesh* represents freedom from this traditional division amongst human beings. It is also a symbol of Sikh spirituality as many holy men in history have uncut hair. Most Sikhs believe that by not cutting any hair on the body they are leaving it in tact, just as God intended. Many Sikh men keep their hair tidy by wearing a turban.

KANGA – a small wooden comb. The *Kanga* symbolises the discipline needed to keep the Sikh faith. This is because in Indian religious tradition, matted hair symbolises withdrawing from the world, which Sikhs do not agree with. Therefore, it is important for Sikhs to use the *Kanga* to keep their hair (*Kesh*) clean and free from a matted condition.

KARA – a steel bracelet. This circular bracelet represents the circle of life – birth and rebirth. The symbol of the circular wheel is common to all Indian religions. The *Kara* also symbolises submission to the 'eternal way', which like God, has no beginning or end. For many Sikhs, the *Kara* also acts as a conscience. It reminds Sikhs of their *Khalsa* vows if they are about to do something wrong. The *Kara* is worn on the wrist and is sometimes described as half a handcuff, the other half being attached to God.

KIRPAN – a small sword. This is sometimes referred to as the 'sword of mercy' and represents defence of all people against tyranny. It should only be used to uphold righteousness in extreme circumstances. The *Kirpan* also has a spiritual meaning. It is a weapon that cuts through ignorance (the Indian word is *avidya*) and therefore represents God, as it is God who ultimately destroys human ignorance or spiritual blindness.

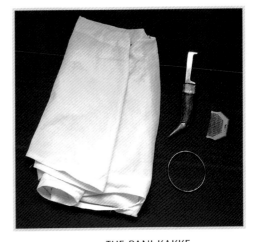

THE PANJ KAKKE
These four symbols, together with the Kesh, make up the Panj Kakke. They remind Sikhs of their faith and commitment.

KACHERA – underwear. Sikhs originally wore these shorts when going into battle. They were far more practical than the traditional *dhoti* (a long strip of white cloth). The *Kachera* represent control of lust, one of the five vices according to Sikhism (see page 17). They do not symbolise chastity, as Sikhs believe this is unnatural. However, they do stand for faithfulness in marriage.

Scriptures

The Sikhs' holiest scripture is called the *Guru Granth Sahib*. The *Guru Granth Sahib* plays a very important role in the lives of all Sikhs.

The book is a compilation of *shabads* composed by six of the Sikh Gurus, plus others written by Hindu and Muslim saints whose views matched those of Sikhs. There are 5,894 *shabads* in the *Guru Granth Sahib*.

A GRANTHI READING THE GURU GRANTH SAHIB

The Sikhs' holiest scripture became known as the *Guru Granth Sahib* following Guru Tegh Bahadur's announcement that it should become their living Guru. The *granthi* is responsible for looking after the *Guru Granth Sahib*.

COMPILING THE GURU GRANTH SAHIB

In 1604 Guru Arjan, the fifth Guru, collected together the writings of the first four Gurus and, adding his own, compiled the *Adi Granth*. The word Adi means 'first' and Granth means 'book'. This scripture was installed in the Harmandir Sahib in the same year. In 1706, the tenth Guru, Guru Gobind Singh, added the writings of Guru Tegh Bahadur and declared that the *Adi Granth* should become Sikhs' living Guru. The book became known as the *Guru Granth Sahib*. 'Sahib' is a word used in India to show respect.

THE GURU GRANTH SAHIB

The *Guru Granth Sahib* has 1,430 pages. Each copy is identical in the way its pages are set out. Therefore, a particular hymn in the book always begins at the same place on the same page no matter where the book is being read. The book is written in a form of Punjabi called Gurmukhi that was popularised and developed by Guru Angad. The word means 'from the Guru's mouth' and Sikhs believe that the scripture contains the actual words of the Gurus. The *Guru Granth Sahib* was copied out by hand until 1852 when the first printed edition appeared. However, no words can be changed in the book and no one is allowed to print copies of the book, except a special Sikh organisation based in Amritsar.

USING THE GURU GRANTH SAHIB IN WORSHIP

In all gurdwaras and at special times in the personal and community life of Sikhs, the *Guru Granth Sahib* is read continuously. This is called the Akhand Path (see page 19).

The *Guru Granth Sahib* is given the utmost respect. It is treated with a reverence that Sikhs would have shown to the Gurus during their lifetime. It holds the highest authority and Sikhs bow down in front of the book when attending the gurdwara.

THE DASAM GRANTH Guru Gobind Singh was a wonderful poetic writer, but did not include any of his writings in the *Guru Granth Sahib*. So in 1734, 26 years after his death, a close companion, Bhai Mani Singh, compiled his writings. This compilation became known as the *Dasam Granth* (collection of the tenth Guru).

RESPECTING THE GURU GRANTH SAHIB
To show his respect the *granthi* carries the *Guru Granth Sahib* on his head into the *darbar* hall (see page 18).

Key beliefs

BELIEFS ABOUT GOD

Sikh beliefs about God cannot be separated from Sikh views about human relationships. A Sikh cannot love God and not love his or her fellow human beings.

Sikhs believe in one God, known by different names, for all humanity. There are many names for God in the *Guru Granth Sahib*, including ones commonly associated with Hindu and Muslim traditions. For Sikhs, God has a personal dimension or *saguna*, which means they believe God is present everywhere and in everything. God is *sarguna nirguna* (transcendent, or above everything) and, unlike some Hindu conceptions of God, never takes a human form. God can be experienced, but is beyond human understanding.

Nevertheless, Sikhs have some particular names for God. Two names traditionally used in worship are: *Sat Nam* (the true name, sometimes translated 'the eternal reality') and *Waheguru* ('wonderful lord' or 'praise to the Guru'). Sikhs believe that God made the world over a period of time and that creation evolved slowly from lower to higher forms of life. From air came water, from water lower forms of life emerged, which in turn led to the formation of plants, birds and animals. Finally, human beings were created as the highest form of life. The basic Sikh belief about God is found in the *Mool Mantra*, the verse which begins every section of the *Guru Granth Sahib*.

MOOL MANTRA	ENGLISH TRANSLATION
Ik	There is but one God
Onkar	God is all-pervading
Satnam	God's Name is everlasting
Karta	God is the Creator
Purukh	God is present throughout Creation
Nirbhao	God fears nothing
Nirvair	God is without enmity
Akal-Murat	God's existence is immortal
Ajuni	God is not born, nor does God die; God is beyond the cycle of birth and death
Swe-Bhang	God is self-illuminated
Gur-Prasad	God is realised through the grace of the Guru

THE GOAL OF LIFE

Guru Nanak taught that everything that happens does so according to *hukam* (God's will).

According to Sikhism, the goal of life is for a person to progress along a spiritual scale from *manmukh*, or 'self-centred', to *gurmukh*, or 'God-centred'. Sikhs use the word *haumai* to describe the natural state of people which results in *manmukh*. *Manmukh* is caused by *maya*, which means delusion. For example, people are often deluded by the attractions of the material world – money, success, physical attraction. These are not bad in themselves, but can become so if people grow attached to them or if they become all important in their lives. Sikhs believe in reincarnation (see page 29), and becoming attached to *maya* means that a person will suffer constant rebirths. It is *maya* that makes humans ignorant of the will of God.

(see page 29)

PRAYING
Sikhs include prayer as part of their everyday life. This helps them to keep God in mind.

THE FIVE VICES

A mind of a *manmukh* gives rise to the five vices, which are lust, anger, greed, worldly attachment and pride. Sikhs aim to become *gurmukh* (God-centred) through a spiritual path of *nam simran* (keeping God constantly in mind) and *sewa* (selfless service on behalf of others), and so become *mukti* (spiritually liberated) which breaks the cycle of rebirths.

THE FIVE VICES:
1. Lust
2. Anger
3. Greed
4. Worldly attachment
5. Pride

SILENT PRAYER
This Sikh woman in New Mexico prays to God by meditating. Meditation helps to focus the worshipper's mind and to become *mukti* (spiritually liberated).

The gurdwara and worship

THE MEANING OF GURDWARA

The word gurdwara means 'the doorway to the Guru'. Gurdwaras can be beautiful buildings, like the Harmandir Sahib, but they can also be humble houses. Any place where the *Guru Granth Sahib* is kept becomes a gurdwara.

Outside India today there are purpose-built gurdwaras, often with a beautiful dome. Others may be converted churches or cinemas. However, what they all have in common is the Sikh flag, the *Nishan Sahib*, which flies outside.

THE NISHAN SAHIB

This is a saffron-coloured flag that always has the *Khanda* on it. The *Khanda* reflects some of the essential ideas within Sikhism. The symbol gets its name from the double-edged sword that stands for Divine Knowledge. It is said this knowledge can cleave, or separate, truth from falsehood. The circle around the *khanda* is called the *chakar*. This symbolises the eternal nature of God and the oneness and equality of humanity. The *chakar* is surrounded by two *Kirpans*. These swords symbolise the concepts of *peeri* (spiritual power) and *meeri* (worldly authority) introduced by Guru Hargobind. The two concepts emphasise how a Sikh should remember God and also contribute to society.

DARBAR HALL

The most important function of a gurdwara is as a place of worship. So, the main focus is on the prayer or *darbar* hall. This is where the *Guru Granth Sahib* is read. It is placed on a decorated throne that is on a dais called the *manji sahib* at the front of the *darbar* hall. The *Guru Granth Sahib* is kept covered by a cloth called a *rumala* when it is not being read. Above the *Guru Granth Sahib* is a canopy called a *chanani*. The *granthi*, the person who looks after the *Guru Granth Sahib*, reads out loud from the scripture. He or she waves a *chauri*, which is like a fly whisk, over the *Guru Granth Sahib* from time to time. This is a symbol of respect for the authority and wisdom of the scripture.

THE AKHAND PATH

Sikhs, and anyone else who wants to worship God, can visit a gurdwara. Some gurdwaras are even open 24 hours a day. People go to pray and listen to the Akhand Path.

The Akhand Path is a continuous reading of the scripture that takes 48 hours to complete. It is a permanent feature of Sikh worship. In smaller gurdwaras the Akhand Path may only take place at weekends. The *granthi* reads for two hours and is then replaced by the next reader. The Akhand Path always takes place at *gurpurbs* and festivals (see pages 22–23). Families also arrange for a continuous reading to mark special times such as births, marriages and deaths.

When a Sikh enters the *darbar* hall, he or she bows down in front of the *Guru Granth Sahib* as a mark of respect and to show humility. Then they offer a donation of money or food. Following this he or she sits and listens to the reading. Men and women usually sit on separate sides of the *darbar* hall.

READING FROM THE GURU GRANTH SAHIB

The *granthi* leads the morning and afternoon service in the gurdwara by reading from the *Guru Granth Sahib*. However, during the 48-hour Akhand Path readers swap over because the words must be spoken clearly.

KARAH PARSHAD

Karah parshad is a blessed food made from flour, water, sugar and ghee (refined butter). During services at the gurdwara it is offered to each person, including any visitors. This special food is offered as a sign of God's blessing and love. For Sikhs, the acceptance of *karah parshad* is a recognition of the equality of all human beings. When a person enters a gurdwara they leave their social status or class behind them.

LANGAR

Langar, or 'free kitchen', is an essential feature of all gurdwaras. *Langar* also refers to the free meal that is offered to everyone, even to visitors. People sit at the same level on the floor to eat the meal. *Langar* is a very practical and symbolic way of showing the Sikh belief in equality and the importance of *sewa* (selfless service on behalf of others).

DAYS FOR WORSHIP

Sikhs do not have a special day of the week for worship; every day is sacred. Nevertheless, outside India many Sikhs tend to go to services on either Saturdays or Sundays. A service at the weekend can last for five or six hours and includes a meal for everyone. The congregation sing *shabads* from the *Guru Granth Sahib* to music played on *tabla* (drums) and a harmonium. This part of the service is called *kirtan*. Anybody can perform *kirtan*, but usually it is the *ragees* (professional musicians) who play and sing.

RAGEES
The *ragees* provide music
and sing during part of the
prayer service called *kirtan*.

After this, a *shabad* composed by Guru Amar Das, called 'Anand Sahib', is recited. The congregation stands with their hands folded while a prayer called the *ardas* is said. After the *ardas* the congregation sits down. The *granthi* then opens the *Guru Granth Sahib* at random and reads a *shabad* from that page. This is called the *hukam* or 'message for the day'. During the service *karah parshad* is distributed to everyone present. People usually stay for *langar* afterwards.

COMMUNITY CENTRE

As well as a place of worship, the gurdwara acts as a community centre. Many large gurdwaras even have rooms for travellers to stay in. In fact, the gurdwara provides food and shelter for any one in need irrespective of their faith. Many also hold Punjabi classes for children. This is so they can learn and begin to understand the *Guru Granth Sahib*, as well as speak the first language of their family. The children also learn to sing the *shabads* from the *Guru Granth Sahib*.

Music plays an important role in the Sikh tradition. All the Gurus thought that music helped people come closer to God. Therefore, many gurdwaras hold music lessons for children and young people. They are taught to play the two most commonly used instruments, the harmonium and the *jori* (two small drums), as well as the *sitar* and *tabla*.

A PUNJABI LESSON
Some gurdwaras provide Punjabi lessons for children so that they can begin to read the *Guru Granth Sahib*.

Sikh festivals

There are two types of Sikh festival. These are the *gurpurbs*, which are holy days in honour of a Guru, and *jorhmelas* or 'fairs'. The latter are important Sikh celebrations that coincide with Hindu festivals. The main ones are *Baisakhi* and *Diwali*.

CELEBRATING GURU NANAK'S BIRTHDAY

During this *gurpurb* Sikh's display pictures of Guru Nanak who was born on 15 April 1469.

GURPURBS

Gurpurbs celebrate events in the Gurus' lives. The main ones are the birthdays of Guru Nanak and Guru Gobind Singh, and the martyrdoms of Guru Arjan and Guru Tegh Bahadur.

The celebration of all the festivals includes the Akhand Path, (see page 19). The reading is timed to finish on the morning of the festival day. *Shabads* are sung and lectures are given on the significance of the day. In the *darbar* hall, *karah parshad* (blessed food) is distributed and *langar* is served. Sometimes banners are hung outside the gurdwara and street processions take place.

REPRESENTING THE PANJ PIARE

Five Sikh men, who represent the Panj Piare, lead the street processions during the celebration of Guru Gobind Singh's birthday.

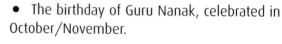

The most important *gurpurbs* are:

- The birthday of Guru Nanak, celebrated in October/November.

- The birthday of Guru Gobind Singh, celebrated in December/January.
A central feature of these celebrations is the procession through the streets. This is led by five people who represent the Panj Piare (see pages 10–11). They are followed by a decorated float that contains the *Guru Granth Sahib*. Large crowds follow singing *shabads* written by the Guru whose birthday they are celebrating.

- The martyrdoms of Guru Arjan and Guru Tegh Bahadur are celebrated in May/June and November/December respectively.

JORHMELAS

Sikh festivals originated with Guru Amar Das. The two most widely celebrated festivals are *Baisakhi* and *Diwali*.

BAISAKHI

Baisakhi celebrates the founding of the *Khalsa* by Guru Gobind Singh in 1699. The festival is usually celebrated on 13 April. In big cities, such as Birmingham in England, there are huge processions and celebrations, including Bhangra music and dancing. A central part of the celebrations is the renewal of the *Nishan Sahib*, the Sikh flag flown outside the gurdwara (see page 18). The flag, and the saffron coloured cloth that is wrapped around the flagpole, are taken down and the flagpole is washed in yoghurt to symbolise purity. The flagpole is then dressed in new cloth and a new flag.

RENEWING THE NISHAN SAHIB
During *Baisakhi,* the *Nishan Sahib* and cloth surrounding the flagpole are changed.

DIWALI

Diwali celebrations for Sikhs remember the release from prison of Guru Hargobind, known as *Bandichorrad* in Punjabi. In 1619 the Mughal Emperor Jahangir imprisoned the Guru. Subsequently, the Emperor found the charges against the Guru to be false and ordered his release at *Diwali* time. The Guru refused to go unless those imprisoned with him were also set free. The Emperor agreed to set free as many as could hold on to the Guru's cloak as they passed out of the narrow gateway of the prison. The Guru had a very long cloak made and he managed to free all 52 prisoners. The Guru arrived in Amritsar on *Diwali* Day and the city, along with the Harmandir Sahib, was decorated with clay lamps (*divas*) to welcome him. Today, the city is illuminated by traditional lamps and electric lights. Lights are also used to decorate gurdwaras and people's homes in many countries throughout the world.

Sacred places

Pilgrimage is not a requirement in Sikhism as it is in some religions. This is because the Gurus rejected a lot of outward rituals usually associated with religion. For example, it says in the *Guru Granth Sahib*: 'True pilgrimage consists in contemplation of the name of God and the cultivation of inner knowledge.' However, there are sacred places that Sikhs regard as very important and they try to visit them.

THE HARMANDIR SAHIB
The Harmandir Sahib is also known as the 'Golden Temple'. The Temple was completed by Guru Arjan in 1601.

THE HARMANDIR SAHIB, AMRITSAR

Amritsar, which means 'pool of nectar', is a town in the Punjab. It was here that Guru Ram Das began building a place for Sikhs to congregate in 1577. Guru Arjan, the fifth Guru, finished the Temple in 1601. The Harmandir Sahib, or Golden Temple, is a symbol of Sikh history and spiritual tradition. There are entrances on all four sides of the building showing that everyone is welcome. Guru Arjan said: 'My faith is for the people of all castes and all creeds from whichever direction they come and to whichever direction they bow.' The first edition of the *Guru*

Granth Sahib was installed there in 1604. During the reign of Maharaja Ranjit Singh the doors and domes were decorated with gold leaf. The Temple has been damaged several times, perhaps the most serious of which occurred in 1984 after a military invasion by the Indian Army.

THE FIVE TAKHTS

Part of the complex of the Harmandir Sahib houses the *Akal Takht* (eternal throne). This was founded by Guru Hargobind and is one of the five Takhts (thrones). These are seats of worldly authority, where leaders of the Takhts make decisions affecting the Sikh community.

The remaining four Takhts are actually gurdwaras. All four have a connection with the life of Guru Gobind Singh.

The **Patna Sahib** is the place where Guru Gobind Singh was born in 1666. It is situated in Patna, the capital of the northern Indian state of Bihar. The **Keshgarh Sahib** is located in Anandpur in the Punjab and is where the *Khalsa* was founded by Guru Gobind Singh in 1699. Some of the Guru's weapons are housed there. The most precious article is a *khanda* (double-edged sword) that belonged to the Guru, which he used to prepare *amrit* for the *Khalsa* initiation ceremony. The **Damdama Sahib** at Talwandi Sabo, near Bhatinda in the Punjab, is where Guru Gobind Singh lived for a year in order to complete the final version of the *Guru Granth Sahib* in 1705. The **Hazur Sahib** is situated in Nanded, in the central Indian state of Maharashtra, and is the place where Guru Gobind Singh died. The inner room of the gurdwara is built over the place where the Guru was cremated.

INSIDE THE KESHGARH SAHIB

The Keshgarh Sahib is in Anandpur, where the *Khalsa* was founded by Guru Gobind Singh. Some of the weapons that belonged to him, including *chakars* and *Kirpans*, can be seen there.

Family life and values

THE IMPORTANCE OF MARRIAGE

The Gurus taught that family life is very important, and marriage is essential to maintain family life. By being married a Sikh can develop the qualities of contentment, charity, kindness, happiness and humility.

Sikhism rejects the idea that a person needs to isolate themselves from the world for spiritual reasons. Sikh spirituality emphasises the importance of living life as part of the world. In particular it stresses that the responsibilities of marriage bring about spiritual balance to life. Sikhs therefore balance worship and meditation with *kirat karna* (honest work) and *sewa* (selfless service on behalf of others).

Guru Nanak said: 'Wandering ascetics, warriors, celebates, sannyasins (Hindus who have withdrawn from the world), none of them obtains the fruit of liberation without performing *sewa*.'

A FAMILY MEAL
Family life through marriage is important for Sikhs. They believe it spiritually balances their lives.

KIRAT KARNA (honest work)

Sikhs believe in the value of all work. Often jobs like cleaning people's shoes in the gurdwara or washing dishes may seem very simple and unimportant. However, such jobs remind Sikhs of humility. They believe this helps to combat self-centredness, which is a major cause of spiritual unhappiness. Sikhs should try to earn their living by honest means. They should work hard and only take what they need for themselves.

VAND CHHAKNA

Sikhs should also practise *vand chhakna*, which means sharing their wealth for the benefit of the community.

In this sense 'wealth' may mean giving money, or giving time, or using skills or expertise to help others. It involves helping everyone, not only other Sikhs. For example, Sikhs may share 'themselves' by welcoming the poor and needy to the gurdwara and providing them with *langar*. However, it would not be possible for somebody to rely on this forever

VAND CHHAKNA
Sharing their wealth is
something that Sikhs learn
to do from a young age.

as this would not aid them spiritually. Sikhs believe it is important to be able to make a contribution to the world.

For many Sikhs, even from an early age, preparing and serving *langar* are important experiences from which they can learn about *sewa*.

THE STORY OF LALO AND BHAGO

On one of his journeys, Guru Nanak stayed with a carpenter in a place called Emnabad. The carpenter's name was Lalo. A local wealthy man called Bhago decided to give a feast and invited all around, including Guru Nanak. However, the Guru did not attend and when asked why Nanak replied that he would rather eat the carpenter's bread because it had been earned by honest work, whereas Bhago's great feast had been the result of exploitation of the poor. Nanak said that the bread had been stained by the blood of the poor. When Bhago protested, Guru Nanak took a piece of Lalo's bread and a piece of Bhago's bread and squeezed them both. Milk dripped from Lalo's bread while Bhago's dripped with blood. Bhago then repented and devoted the rest of his life to those in need.

EQUALITY

The Gurus' teachings about God led to a view of the equality of all humanity. These teachings were truly revolutionary in their time and some would say they are still so today. The bestowing of the name 'Singh' and 'Kaur' on men and women respectively by Guru Gobind Singh, indicates the importance of equal status of men and women.

Life ceremonies

There are four ceremonies that mark important stages in the life of a Sikh. These are: the naming of a child, *Amrit Sanskar* (initiation into the *Khalsa*, see page 11), marriage, and death. All Sikh ceremonies are held in the presence of the *Guru Granth Sahib*.

THE NAMING CEREMONY
This naming ceremony is taking place in a gurdwara, but it can also be held at home. The ceremony often takes place a few weeks after the birth of a baby.

THE NAMING CEREMONY

This ceremony takes place a few weeks after the birth of a baby. A baby is seen as a gift from God. The naming ceremony is often included as part of a normal service in the gurdwara, or it can be held separately either in the gurdwara or at the family's home.

After prayers the child's name is taken from the first letter of the *vak* (a passage in the *Guru Granth Sahib* that is read after opening the book at random). A girl's name is followed by 'Kaur' and a boy's by 'Singh' as begun by Guru Gobind Singh.

MARRIAGE

Marriage in Sikhism is seen as a spiritual state of being and not just a social contract. This is because the Gurus proclaimed marriage as the ideal state for spiritual development. The love between husband and wife is compared with the love and longing of the human soul for God. Guru Ram Das composed the marriage hymn, the *Lavan*, in which he said that awe, love, restraint and harmony are as important for the relationship in marriage as they are between devotee and God. Most Sikh marriages are assisted marriages. This means that parents introduce the young man to the young woman or vice versa. Nevertheless, a marriage cannot take place unless the couple agree to it. A Sikh marriage is seen as more than the joining of two people, it is a union of two families. They are involved in every stage of the marriage.

Anand Karaj

Anand Karaj (the Sikh marriage ceremony) means 'ceremony of bliss'. The ceremony takes place in the presence of the *Guru Granth Sahib*. The groom sits in front of the holy book. The bride is escorted by a female companion and together they sit beside the groom. A prayer is said and the couple are reminded of their duties to one another. They nod to say they will fulfil their marital duties and the end of the groom's scarf is placed in the bride's hand. Then the four verses of the *Lavan* are read.

At the end of each verse the groom leads the bride around the *Guru Granth Sahib* in a clockwise direction, while the *ragees* sing the verse that has just been read. After the fourth circling of the scripture the couple are married. The marriage ceremony ends with the *ardas* prayer.

DEATH

Sikhs believe that death is according to God's will. They are encouraged to see death as a natural part of life. In the scripture it says: 'The dawn of a new day is the message of a sunset. Earth is not your permanent home.'

ANAND KARAJ
During the marriage ceremony the couple are given gifts.

REINCARNATION

Sikhs believe in reincarnation, which means the soul moves into another living body. This is often compared to going to sleep at the end of the day and waking up the next morning. However, it is still recognised that loved ones will feel grief and sorrow. Before they go to sleep, Sikhs read *Kirtan Sohila*, which is also the prayer used at funerals.

CREMATION

Sikhs normally cremate their dead. Before the funeral the body is washed and, if the person had been initiated into the *Khalsa*, dressed in the Panj Kakke. The body is taken to a crematorium in a procession. At the crematorium, the *granthi* leads the mourners in a reading of the *Kirtan Sohila*. The congregation is reminded of the words in the reading relating to the aim of life which is: 'Know the real purpose of being here, gather up treasure under the guidance of the *Sat Guru* [true Guru, or God]. Make your mind God's home. If God abides with you undisturbed you will not be reborn.' Finally, the *ardas* is said to ask for peace for the dead person's soul. Many Sikhs travel from around the world to scatter the ashes of the dead in the Punjab. They are usually put into a river or stream.

FUNERAL PREPARATIONS
After the body is prepared it is moved from the house to be cremated.

Sikhs are not allowed to put up headstones or other memorials. This is because people should be remembered for the good things they did during their life.

Key questions and answers

WHAT IS SIKHISM? Sikhism is the youngest of the major religions and dates from the fifteenth century CE. The origins of Sikhism lie in the teachings of Guru Nanak and his successors.

HOW MANY SIKHS ARE THERE WORLDWIDE? 16 million (estimated).

WHAT DO SIKHS BELIEVE? Sikhs believe in one God, often called *Sat Nam* or *Waheguru*. For Sikhs, God is present everywhere and in everything, but is beyond human understanding. The basic Sikh belief about God is found in the *Mool Mantra* (see page 16). Sikhs are initiated into the *Khalsa* during *Amrit Sanskar*, and make vows to show commitment to their faith (see pages 10–12). Members of the *Khalsa* wear the Panj Kakke, or 5 Ks (see pages 12–13). Sikhs believe that all humans are equal.

WHAT ARE THE SIKH TEACHINGS AND VALUES? Sikhs follow the teachings of the ten Gurus – Guru Nanak, Guru Angad, Guru Amar Das, Guru Ram Das, Guru Arjan, Guru Hargobind, Guru Har Rai, Guru Har Krishan, Guru Tegh Bahadur and Guru Gobind Singh (see pages 6–7). Sikhs are taught the importance of family life, to live life as part of the world, *kirat karna* (honest work) and *vand chhakna* (sharing wealth for the benefit of others) (see pages 26–27).

WHAT ARE THE SIKH SCRIPTURES CALLED? The holiest Sikh scripture is the *Guru Granth Sahib*. It is a collection of *shabads* (hymns) written by six of the Gurus, plus others written by Hindu and Muslim saints (see pages 14–15). The *Guru Granth Sahib* is kept in the Sikhs' holy building, called a gurdwara.

WHERE DO SIKHS WORSHIP? Sikhs worship in a gurdwara (see pages 18–21). Gurdwaras can be any building, but they all have a flag flying outside, called a *Nishan Sahib*. Gurdwaras have a *darbar* hall, where people pray and eat *langar*. The *Guru Granth Sahib* is kept in the *darbar* hall on a dais, called the *manji sahib*, and is covered by a *rumala* when not in use. The *granthi* looks after and cares for the *Guru Granth Sahib*.

WHAT ARE THE SIKH FESTIVALS? There are two types of Sikh festival: *gurpurbs* and *jorhmelas*. *Gurpurbs* include: the birthdays of Guru Nanak and Guru Gobind Singh, and the martyrdoms of Guru Arjan and Guru Tegh Bahadur. *Jorhmelas* include: *Baisakhi* and *Diwali*.

Glossary

AKHAND PATH Continuous reading of the *Guru Granth Sahib* from beginning to end.

AMRIT SANSKAR Initiation into the *Khalsa*.

ANAND KARAJ The Sikh marriage ceremony.

ARDAS Formal Sikh prayer that begins and/or ends every ritual. It has three parts, which encourage Sikhs to remember the Gurus, the teachings of the *Guru Granth Sahib* and to ask for God's blessing.

BAISAKHI Second month of the Hindu calendar and the spring harvest festival in the Punjab. Celebrated by Sikhs in April to remember the forming of the *Khalsa*.

CASTE The ancient Hindu system governing social structure which determines a person's 'class'.

DHOTI A piece of cloth wrapped around the loins. A traditional form of dress among Hindu men.

DIWALI A major Hindu festival celebrated in October/November. Sikhs remember that from the time of Guru Amar Das the Gurus summoned them to gather together at *Diwali* and *Baisakhi*. In 1577 the foundation stone of the Harmandir Sahib was laid at *Diwali* and Guru Hargobind was released from prison in 1619.

DOWRY The property or money given to the husband as part of a marriage agreement.

GRANTHI One who cares for or looks after the *Guru Granth Sahib*. There is no priesthood in Sikhism.

GURDWARA Sikh temple. Literally 'the doorway to the Guru'.

GURMUKH God-centred.

GURMUKHI The written form of Punjabi used in Sikh scriptures, literally meaning 'from the mouth of the Guru'.

GURU GRANTH SAHIB The Sikh holy scripture.

HARMANDIR SAHIB Literally, temple of God, sometimes called Darbar Sahib (Divine Court). It is commonly known as the Golden Temple.

HAUMAI Self-centredness. The major natural spiritual defect that results in *manmukh*.

HUKAM An Arabic word meaning 'divine order' or the 'will of God'.

JANAM SAKHIS The 'life story' of Guru Nanak.

JAPJI The first of Guru Nanak's *shabads* (hymns). A Sikh should meditate on *japji* every morning.

KARA A steel band worn on the right wrist.

KHALSA The community of the pure created by Guru Gobind Singh in 1699.

KHANDA Double-edged sword used in the initiation ceremony. Also, the symbol on the Sikh flag.

KIRAT KARNA Earning one's living by honest means.

KIRTAN SOHILA Evening prayer also read at funerals and when the *Guru Granth Sahib* is covered by the *rumala*.

LANGAR Guru's kitchen. The gurdwara dining hall and the food served in it. Everyone, no matter what his or her social status, is welcome.

LAVAN Marriage hymn composed by Guru Ram Das.

MANMUKH Self-centred as opposed to *gurmukh*, God-centred. *Manmukh* occurs when someone is dominated by *haumai*.

MOOL MANTRA The basic statement of belief about God at the beginning of every section of the *Guru Granth Sahib*.

MUKTI Spiritually liberated.

NAM SIMRAN Keeping God constantly in mind.

NISHAN SAHIB The Sikh flag flown outside a gurdwara.

PANJ PIARE The five beloved ones. The first to be initiated into the *Khalsa*. Representatives perform the initiation today.

SAT NAM The true name. A popular name for God in Sikhism.

SEWA Selfless service on behalf of others.

VAND CHHAKNA Sharing one's time, talents and earnings with those who are less fortunate.

WAHEGURU 'Wonderful lord'. A popular name for God in Sikhism.

Index